BANNERS & BRASS
Images of Durham Miners' Gala

Photographs by Dave Jamieson

The authors of this book have made every effort to ensure that the content is factually correct at the time of going to print. It does not represent the views of any individual or organisation. If you have any comments please contact County Durham Books so that they may be considered for any future editions.

FOREWORD

Since it first took place in 1871, the Durham Miners' Gala, or the Big Meeting as it is also known, has traditionally been a source of pride and inspiration for the miners of the Durham coalfield, a symbol of their unity and strength.

At the height of the mining industry, during the first half of the twentieth century, the Gala attracted huge crowds and for one day each year, the streets of Durham were filled with processions of marching bands and colliery banners, passing political leaders who watched from the balcony of the Royal County Hotel. Tens of thousands of County Durham people attended including miners and their families.

This book contains images by Dave Jamieson, taken over the last three decades and aims to illustrate the atmosphere and tradition of this unique event. It is by no means a complete record but shows the changing face of the Durham Miners' Gala now that the pits have gone, and how it is developing, with the support of Durham County Council, into a county and regional festival.

Young or old, *Banners & Brass* will I hope, rekindle your very own Gala Day memories.

Councillor Albert Nugent
Leader, Durham County Council

DURHAM MINERS' GALA: A BRIEF HISTORY

The mining industry has long been associated with unionism where gatherings and meetings of workers were held to demonstrate a united front to leaders and mine owners in a bid to improve their pay and working conditions.

One such union, The Durham Miners' Mutual Association (DMA) was formed on 20 November 1869 after a meeting of local mining delegates at the Market Hotel in Durham's market place. It was formed as a benefit society, with the aim of improving the running of the collieries and protecting members from injustice. In its early years much work was done towards improving conditions for miners.

The 1st Annual Gala of the DMA was held in Wharton Park, Durham City, on August 12th 1871 and 5,000 people attended. It moved to its current location on the Durham Racecourse in 1873 and has been held there ever since. There have been very few years when there hasn't been a Gala at all, the two world wars being two of the notable cancellations.

Traditionally, a week before the Gala, the DMA secretary would send out a notice to the collieries urging good attendance. People were encouraged to come and show their support, to march with 'their' banners and bands and demonstrate to employers that they took their welfare seriously; that they were united in their cause. It was generally believed that a good attendance at the Gala had a positive influence on the year ahead.

To give further incentive, some collieries paid Gala Day attendance money to the men who went into Durham and those who deliberately failed to give their support were 'hauled over the coals'. The Gala became a customary holiday, taken at the area union's own request, and was not included in the list of statutory paid holidays.

Many Gala Day procedures and traditions have been developed over the years with many still followed today despite the demise of the collieries and associated mining communities.

One of the most symbolic sights of the Gala has always been that of the colliery banners being paraded through the streets of Durham accompanied by brass bands and crowds of eager supporters. The north east has a long history of carrying banners in processions, beginning in medieval times when trades' guilds would represent themselves with banners.

Banners were used by mine 'lodges' (the workers organisations) of individual collieries to express their beliefs and convictions. They usually depicted religious themes, politics and mining related issues and bore mottos and images of famous leaders. Bright and colourful, the banners were originally designed to be noticed and attract the attention of the authorities of the day. They are still a great source of local pride today.

Lodges traditionally draped black crepe across the top of the banner if there had been any miners killed at their colliery since the last Gala and occasionally, banners would be draped in memory of departed politicians, union leaders, or other respected figures.

Banners are carried through the streets of Durham accompanied by brass bands. When there were pits in the County, lodges would book their own band for the day, either from the local colliery or from further a-field. In the early years the DMA provided funding towards the cost of paying bandsmen on the day.

The order in which the lodges parade through the city depends on which ones arrive first. Those arriving at Durham Station begin at North Road and march over Framwellgate Bridge, up Silver Street into the Market Place then down across Elvet Bridge before proceeding past the Royal County Hotel and down to the Racecourse. Those from the north and east of the county traditionally approach from Claypath and join the procession in the Market Place. The rest come to Elvet and link into the procession at the Royal County Hotel. Visiting speakers stand on the balcony of the Royal County Hotel to watch the procession go by. Once at the Racecourse, each lodge stands its banner in an established location at the edge of the field - the same place each year. The banners are a rallying point for the men, women and children who march with them.

'Gresford' (the miners' special tune) is played before the speeches begin from the platforms. In the past, union officials would report on the current state of affairs and this was a chance for people to gather around and listen to the words of invited speakers, usually political leaders of the day. In the days before television this was a rare opportunity for people to see their 'heroes' and listen to their words of inspiration.

In time, amusement stalls began to appear around the edge of the field offering refreshments, shooting galleries, boxing contests, photographic galleries, fortune tellers and more recently, full fairground attractions. The Gala has always been a day for family picnics and in the past, women would spend the preceding days baking for the occasion.

An important part of the Gala Day proceedings was the service in Durham Cathedral. At 3pm the Miners' Festival Service was and still is, held in the Cathedral. In the past, three chosen lodges, with their banners and bands, proceed to the Cathedral followed by their supporters. Although there has been some slight variation in the form of the service over the years, a standard format is now followed. The service remembers the men and boys who have died in the pits of the Durham coalfield. A memorial to them was dedicated there on February 22nd 1947.

Usually the prayers, in part or whole, relate to the mining industry and donations are made for mining related good causes.

The end of the service marks the end of the formal Gala proceedings, and there is a general exodus from the city and the Racecourse, as many people begin to make their way home.

Traditionally, the bands, upon their return to the villages, would play through the main streets, followed by the banner and those who accompanied it.

Images of Durham Miners' Gala

1973

A sunny day sees early morning revellers arrive in North Road for the Gala in Durham. Already there to meet them is a man selling pop-star rosettes and union flags.

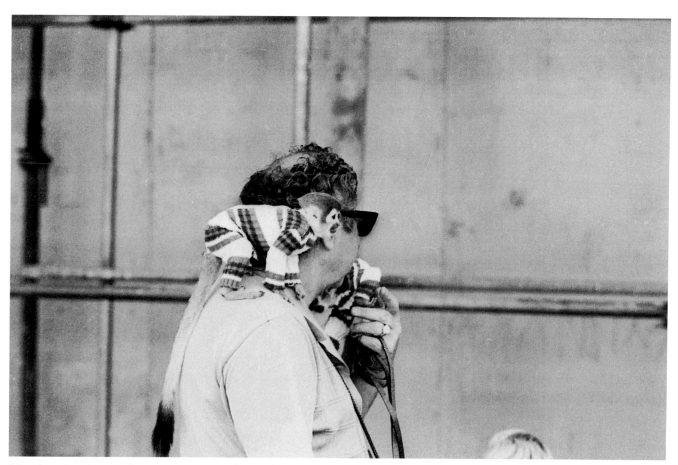

Monkey business. Entertainment of the day included performing monkeys.

The first bands of the day arrive and march across Elvet Bridge towards the Royal County Hotel. People line the route ready for the parade.

Huge crowds march behind the bands and banners on their way to the Racecourse.

In the heat of the sun a proud bandsman gives his best for the dignitaries and public at the Royal County Hotel.

The crowds advance towards the Racecourse with a village jazz band proudly leading them past the dignitaries.

A wee Scot with the band's drummers. Not all bands at the Gala are from County Durham!

With union flag flying, a smiling reveller enjoys the parade.

A happy clapping soul welcomes the bands as they march to Durham Cathedral for the traditional afternoon service.

A young onlooker in daddy's arms shows her allegiance.

A gentleman stops to doff his hat to the dignitaries.

Dancing in the streets. The band goes up-tempo and the girls let themselves go.

Letting their hair down. The girls dance in the July sunshine.

Smiles and waves for Prime Minister Harold Wilson.

Crowds clearly showing the spirit of the Gala.

Well, fancy meeting you! A cheerful lady meets up with old friends.

A gentleman waves on the bands.

The young ones. All dressed up in their 70s gear they were out to enjoy themselves.

Invited dignitaries view the parade from their lofty viewpoint at the Royal County Hotel.

Harold Wilson prepares to address the crowd on the Racecourse.

Members of the public listen to Harold Wilson.

Another year over.

Images of Durham Miners' Gala

1983

It's 1983 and there are huge changes as some pits are closed. Families still turn out in their thousands to enjoy the Big Meeting in Durham. The bands pass by the Royal County Hotel, this time with Neil Kinnock and guests looking on.

Neil Kinnock, leader of the Labour Party at the time, seen here mingling with the crowds.

Michael Foot and his dog Dizzy with Glenys Kinnock to his right, Tony Benn to his left and other Labour stalwarts on the balcony of the Royal County Hotel.

In the mood. Young and older swing along with toy instruments.

Invited guests bring refreshing new sights and sounds and an international flavour to the traditional Gala Day proceedings.

Framed by miners' banners, a balloon seller waits for trade.

"Love is in the air" goes the song, and it certainly seems to have been the case as the Gala draws to an end.

There's always a wide range of activities on offer at the Gala.

Brrr! Just the day for an ice-cream.

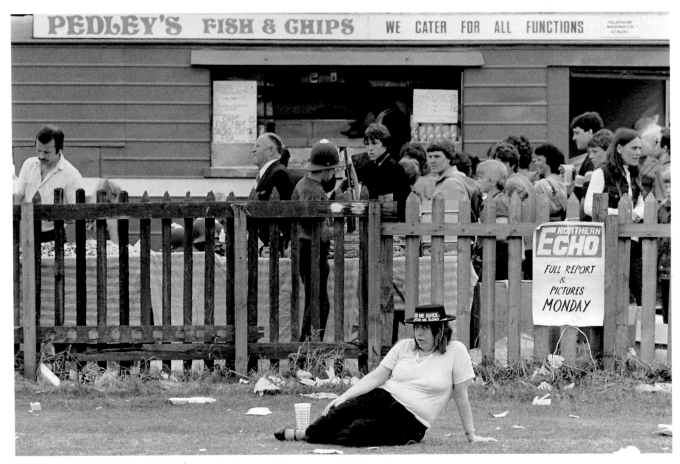

A young lady takes a break.

Beneath the towering Durham Cathedral, Mickey Mouse enjoys the fun of the fair.

Images of Durham Miners' Gala
2005

It's 2005 and the bands and banners are arriving. There are no pits remaining open in the County, but the bands and banners carry on the traditions of the past as they look to the future.

The procession crosses the River Wear beneath the spires of Durham Cathedral and imposing fortifications of the castle.

With a picnic in hand, father and son find peace and solitude away from the crowds, at the deserted boat house beneath Elvet Bridge.

New banners join the old.

The procession passes the Royal County Hotel.

A special note of gratitude to the local Member of Parliament features on the Browney Lodge banner.

Beating out the rhythm, ready for the off.

The banners begin to arrive.

Packed tightly, the bands and banners mingle with the crowd.

Heading towards the Royal County Hotel.

Carried with pride is the banner depicting Peter Lee.

A collection of plates celebrate the former pits of County Durham.

Families gather at the Racecourse ready for the speeches.

A comedy duo keep the public happy.

Crowds relax in the heat of the sun.

"In the shade of the old oak tree". Not quite, but this umbrella came in handy.

A Scottish pipe band enters the ground.

TO THE FUTURE...

In the early part of the twentieth century, when coal mining in County Durham was at its peak and 170,000 miners were employed, the Durham Miners' Gala was in its heyday. With the decline of the mining industry came a decline in the numbers of people attending the Gala. By the 1980s the number of banners attending had dwindled and the 1990s saw an all time low in numbers attending the Gala.

Efforts by the NUM and Durham County Council to develop the Gala for the new generation of County Durham people has seen numbers gradually increasing again and 2006 saw a crowd of around 70,000 people on the Racecourse. As new generations populate County Durham's towns and villages, the focus of the Gala is inevitably shifting away from its original cause; as a show of solidarity and unity amongst the working classes. Whilst still firmly based on the strong and proud traditions of the mining heritage of County Durham, the Gala is evolving and has developed into a multi-cultural family festival whilst still remaining a celebrated tradition amongst County Durham people.